starts

strategically

2 books in 1

1. **Start Thinking**

2. **Strategic Thinking**

Ray Crystal

Strategic Thinking

learn to make smart decisions,

using the right habits to change

your life forever

Ray Crystal

The Systems View

Step 1: The systems thinking experts started unwinding the problem backward.

There were no denying Acme's sales were decreasing by the day and that potentially new and current customers were choosing Acme's competitors as a supplier.

Step 2: Based on what was identified in Step 1,

known as the critical problem, systems thinking experts started digging deeper. What was the most direct reason for the drop in sales?

They concluded that Acme's poor service (the flawed billing and delivery delays) was the direct reason for customer loss.

The direct reason was not hard to guess as these symptoms were the most visible. But what about the indirect reasons behind the poor service?

Step 3: What was causing poor service?

After spending time with Acme employees and talking about their work routines, it turned out the employees were overwhelmed by "special orders."

The amount of regular automated orders had decreased while the amount of these special orders had dramatically increased. Since the billing requirements were also unique, the chances of billing errors also increased and were the cause of the billing issues.

The responsibilities and tasks of the employees had grown, but the number of employees had not.

All these stressful factors' cumulated effect put an increased burden on the service department employees, which resulted in poor service and then resulted in a drop in sales.

Step 4: Step 3 revealed a new, ignored, problematic element in the Acme equation: the special orders. Where were the special orders coming from?

The systems thinking professionals needed the answer to this question, so they turned to the sales manager.

Following the interview, it turned out the manager, to counterbalance the market's hazards and supply sufficiently attractive product packages, had come up with creative and unique packages to increase sales.

He'd congratulated his team's efforts, noting the special pricing and expanded delivery options were both attractive features for new customers.

Step 5: The sales manager

failed to notice how these new "attractive" features were sabotaging, rather than helping, the company's overall success.

The manager admitted the main reason for coming up with new features was the desperate need to find new customers to keep Acme's sales on track.

And thus, the loop closed for Acme. Remember where we started in Step 1? Acme's main problem was customer loss.

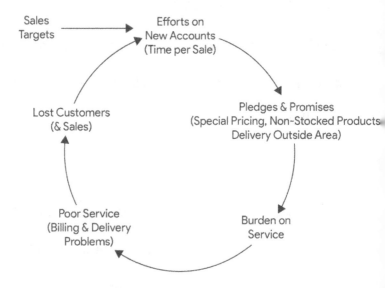

If you read counter-clockwise, starting from "lost customers," you'll see the deductive logic systems thinking experts used to dig deeper and get to the bottom of Acme, Inc.'s issues.

Now start reading clockwise from "sales targets." To meet sales targets, the sales department needed to bring in new customers.

How could they do that?

By outperforming other competitors in the form of special features.

They dumped their innovations onto an unprepared and already busy service department, which caused an even greater division of their attention.

Their frustration and lack of computerized systems led to human errors and, in the grand scheme of things, poor service drove customers away. What did Acme do in response to this?

The sales department saw the poor sales numbers, so they put more effort into overly complicated special packages and caused even more burden on the service employees.

In systems thinking, we call this phenomenon reinforcing feedback, meaning the actions taken reinforced whatever was already going on in the loop.

Before we move on with the story of Acme, Inc., let's take a closer look at how the systems thinking team analyzed the problem differently than the first consulting team.

The original consulting team had focused on the most visible symptoms, considering each point independently from one another. On the other hand, the systems thinking team dug deeper into the problem, starting from the most visible.

The systems thinking view also shed light on the lack of communication between departments (in this case, the sales and service departments) and had them work on solutions together instead of independently trying to fix each department's issues.

The consulting team focused on each part of Acme separately. Simultaneously, the systems thinking experts took a holistic, big-picture view of the company's product mismanagement and then went a level lower to investigate the role of different departments.

Even when they discovered the cause of the problem, the system thinking experts did not separate the two departments involved but instead encouraged a solution through communication and cooperation.

True enough, before we start casting aspersions toward the consultation company, let's take a moment to think about our approaches to solving problems in our own lives. Be honest with yourself and answer these questions:

- **Do I usually approach my problems with a linear or systemic solution?**
- **Why don't I choose to use the systemic approach more often?**

I would assume your answer to the first question to be a "linear solution" rather than a systemic approach.

Most of us think this way, and for a good reason. The majority of our everyday problems don't require deep systemic analysis. If your watch stops, you change the battery. If you're hungry, you eat. If you miss your mom, you call or visit her.

If it rains, you grab your umbrella. I could go on with the list of mundane problems that would make us go nuts if we attempted to solve with a systemic view.

There are, however, some problems in our lives that can't be fixed with a simple "if this then that" approach.

These are the real problems, the deal-breakers (or heartbreakers). Do you feel anxious regularly?

Sure, you can take medication (linear thinking) and numb your anxiety each day. But medication won't heal your anxiety disorder.

You need to take an in-depth, sometimes painful look at why anxiety hits you so hard or regularly.

Do you feel sorry for homeless people?

Sure, you could give them a night in a shelter (linear thinking) and help them have something in their stomach for another day.

But tomorrow, they will be hungry again, without a safe and permanent place to call home. Joining a collective effort to promote the creation of permanent housing for these unfortunate folks would bear more long-lasting results.

I'm not saying I don't take medication to alleviate your pain of today or not give shelter to ease today's struggle. I'm only saying that seeking those solutions won't make your life, or the lives of the homeless, better in the long run.

Long-term explanations usually take a long time, a lot of effort, and sacrifice. Thus, they are naturally less appealing than the instant gratification that we all look for. We are wired that way as humans. In his book Stumbling on Happiness, Dan Gilbert presented the neuroscientific fact that our ability to think about the future developed somewhere in the past three million years and could be attributed to our frontal lobes fast growth.

Before that, our ancestors lived in the "never-ending, present moment."

Given the relatively young age of the thinking brain compared to the "reptilian brain," we can conclude our genetic inclination toward wanting something now rather than later is perfectly understandable.

I know that systems problems are complex.

They are not as common as everyday problems.

The problems they cover often seem too big or too overwhelming.

You don't think you have time or knowledge to expand on this thinking method properly.

It often requires more information, teamwork, and higher-level thinking tools.

Do you have other reasons?

Please add them to this list.

When you are done listing why you shouldn't learn to think in systems, let's examine the list of reasons you should. I'll start with the conclusion of the story of Acme.

Forming Good Habits that Last

You want to be successful. It's the whole reason you've read this book to this point. I applaud you for that.

I assume that you now understand the importance of thinking about the long term in your quest for success. You get that you've got to be disciplined for you to conquer milestone after milestone along your journey.

The only method to move up the ladder of success is by constantly repeating the things that work, one rung at a time. In other words, to succeed, it all comes down to your habits.

If you want to start up a new business or improve your health, you must make sure you have the right habits. The question is, how can you not just replace bad habits with good ones, but also make them permanent?

First, we're going to take a critical look at all the things people get wrong about habits.

Myths about Building Habits

"It takes 21 days for you to form a habit." How many times have you heard that one? Well, that's not the way it goes.

There's no proper research backing that up. Before you argue, reread the last sentence and notice the word 'proper' is in bold letters.

Real research on how time-consuming it takes to form a habit suggests that many variables could affect how long it takes you to form a habit, from your environment to the habit, to your kind of person, among other things.

I guess there's no way to spin that into a great book title, so many people preach that 21 days' hogwash.

You shouldn't be thinking of habits in light of how long it takes you to form them, anyway. If you do that, you'll notice that you're missing out on the point behind creating better habits to begin with: Creating lasting change in your life.

It's a lifestyle thing, not a 21-day fad. You're not going to get results by crossing off each new day on your calendar.

Now that I've sufficiently dashed your dreams of becoming a better person in three weeks, the question becomes, how exactly can you make sure your new habits stick?

Micro Targets and Macro Goals

Let's talk about motivation for a minute. Research has found that if you want to be more disciplined, you would be better off with abstract thinking.

In other words, you can dream big. You can be all about the big picture and forget about the minutiae.

With that said, many people are uncomfortable with making plans they deem too grand, and as such, they get scared of the size of their dreams and their expectations, thinking there's more of a chance to fail than succeed.

Sound familiar?

Lots of research shows that when you are motivated to make something happen by intrinsic elements, versus extrinsic elements like the anticipation of a reward or the fear of punishment, you will be able to stick with your goals and habits.

You will find ways to walk the fine line between being a big dreamer and doing the little things every day that get you closer to that big dream of yours.

That means when you're intrinsically motivated to make your goals happen, you're cool with not having dramatic, overnight changes. It's just going to come over a while.

With all of that said, to create habits that stick, you need to have micro targets and macro goals.

While the goals are the big picture, the targets are the little things you must do each day to make your goal happen.

Targets make it easy for you to stay on course each day. They help you achieve your goal. Here's the best thing about achieving your goal with targets: The best kinds of targets are the shallow ones.

You could commit to writing just 100 words a day if you're an aspiring author. You could write 101, or even go so far as to write 5000 in a day if you're feeling a bit fired up, but the point is you just need to write 100.

As you do this, you're teaching yourself a new habit. Sure, you may only ever write 100 words a day now and then, but for the most part, chances are you're hitting 5 or 10 times that target.

On Plans, Triggers, and Changes in Behavior

Habits and planning go hand in hand. See, most people talk about a new habit they want to adopt, but rarely do you ever hear them mention why they want to make that new habit a thing.

I know it doesn't seem like much; however, this helps you remain motivated every day. You're less likely to stick with it if all you do is think about it.

Also, don't just start in on a new habit without being clear about what you want to achieve. If you do, you will begin to lose your resolve, and you won't be consistent.

Recent research shows that while visualizing positively helps keep you motivated and inspired, it's not enough. It's a matter of what you visualize. You visualize yourself working out, taking stairs instead of the elevator, saying no to junk food, eating healthy, and so on.

This is the way to give your new habit the stickiness you need to achieve your goal.

For another, when you visualize each of the steps you need to take, you find that you're less anxious about it and are more likely to consider it a possible thing for you to stick with your new habit as part of your lifestyle.

Habits You Should Practice Daily to Stay Productive

You need to get habits in place so that when you run out of motivation, they will kick in automatically, and you'll still be on the right track. When you have the habits in place, it's easy to find motivation even if you're not feeling it...

And you won't have to force it. Here are some habits to form that can keep you motivated and productive.

Visualize.

You have no idea just how powerful visualization is.

Take time to visualize your goals and your future at the start of your day, and you will find yourself feeling inspired to push through with your target.

All you need is three minutes a day, using the 3-phase visualization technique. In phase 1, consider what you'd like to be like for you within the next 3 to 5 years.

See what you've done, what you're doing, who you're with, and where you are. In phase 2, see the next 12 months and what they have in store for you.

In phase 3, see what you have to get started on today so that you can make your dreams come true.

Go over your goals.

Do this each day, and last thing before bed. Go over why you're doing what you do and what you need to do to achieve them.

Not only will you feel motivated, but you will also be able to stay focused and have brilliant ideas on how you can get there.

Take cold showers.

If you're having trouble becoming fully awake, or if you're having trouble focusing, then take a cold shower.

Once you do, you feel motivated and ready to perform. Make a habit of cold morning showers. It's not pleasant at first, but when you step out, you're more than ready to take charge of your day.

Just remain calm, do some deep breathing, and detach your mind from how your skin feels.

Give it 15 to 20 seconds, and it will become obvious the cold is not as bad as you dreaded.

Read. Read something. Every day. I find I feel off if I don't get some reading in.

When you read, your brain will have a lot of material to work with and give you fresh new ideas to inspire you to greatness. Make it a habit to read in the morning and the evening.

Use affirmations.

These are messaging you repeat to yourself every day so that you remember what you're trying to achieve.

You can leave yourself notes where you'll see them, keep your affirmations in your wallet, or as a reminder on your phone.

Affirmations are messaged you find motivating and empowering. They can be famous quotes or your mantra.

Make your environment work for you. This will require some adaptability and flexibility on your part, especially when you're in a challenging environment. Your environment will always influence your productivity levels.

Develop the habit of NOW. Got an idea? Go test it out now. Notice there's something you just have to do? Why not now? There's only ever now. You can tell yourself you'll do it later, but the truth is when later rolls around, it will still be now anyway! So why not does it this now so you can use the next now to do something else? That's how to remain productive.

Intellectual Development

The most basic education levels feature a state whereby the students are said to be in Dualism or a state of Received knowledge.

In this primary stage, the learner's understanding is based on either acknowledging fact or disapproving fiction.

Here, knowledge of a concept depends on one's skill to remember the subject's events. The teacher's part is to deliver facts while the learner must learn and relay the facts during an examination.

Their learner is bound to get frustrated as this stage involves getting to know a concept without a factual basis.

This leads to the next level, which is referred to as subjective knowledge. This stage entails the memorizing of all the dimensions relative to a particular subject. However, this is an uphill approach that eventually facilitates understanding that learners possess valuable ideologies even when they are seen to have disparities in argument within themselves, with the tutors, and with the books.

This stage's dangerous threat is that learners are confused by disparity view-point and conception of situations, a condition described as intellectual paralysis.

However, for the ideologies to be applicable in the real world, the learner needs to adopt a particular part of thinking and a different manner of viewing various aspects of life.

This equips the learner with the ability to pick a specific line of thought.

This may be a temporary influence, which is subject to change according to the situation but is more advantageous to the learner than the initial stages of the uncertainty of perception.

This is a highly advanced level of understanding and comprehension and is usually only achieved by a few of the accomplished scholars who can make that level in limited exposure to advanced education levels.

Social Identity Development

This is defined as the mental process through which we perceive or acknowledge our social identities or our status in society.

Every person desires to identify their place in the community. These social groupings are classified as either stigmatized or a dominant cluster.

They serve as platforms for an individual to discover one's social identity and to cultivate a sense of belonging in society.

Researchers in this field have observed the relationship between these processes of perception and the learning process.

According to research, these two pathways share similar characteristics.

In this case, children are observed to exhibit naivety in perspective in the earlier stages of development, for instance, being able to distinguish skin color or other physical attributes but not characterize these attributes to the person's character or personality.

Soon, they become bombarded with external views and experiences that open their minds to the character traits of the most appropriate figures, the best lifestyle trends, and the best insights in life.

These insights are universal, and as such, are many times accepted as exhibiting both stigmatized and dominant characteristics.

These learners challenge these external influences and views when injustices are committed or through interactions with other groups in meaningful ways.

For most people, college is still the first significant interaction with people of diverse social positions, grouped collaborations whereby information and content about specific fields become the motivator for the questioning process.

This process differs according to the stages.

The stigmatized members in society find themselves in the immersion stage.

They try to find comparative avenues to share their experiences with friends and peers, enabling them to curb social anomalies like racism, among other delinquencies in society.

On the other hand, members of dominant groups enter the Disintegration stage.

Here, they face the oppressive history of their group.

Their perception of their identity in society is challenged and disintegrates, forcing them to restructure their manners of understanding and comprehension of their character.

Both processes can bear the pain and extreme guilt and anger feelings.

The individuals who develop continuously can create a positive sense of self during the Internalization and Redefinition stages.

They discover that social realization is only a single aspect of one's entire self.

Many learners at the college level are stuck at the acceptance, immersion, and disintegration phases, which breed more confusion during course evaluation.

This conflict will affect the entire course climate and retard the learning process unless it is absorbed and directed into a beneficial talk about

Course Climate

Learners utilize the course contexts as they work out their developmental activities. It is, therefore, crucial to creating a learning environment that conducive to the learning process.

A study based on the female gender was initially used to draw attention to the learning climate through the "chilly climate" articles, which back in the '80s featured the learning climate for female students appertaining to higher educational levels.

However, research studies have provided conclusive evidence of an unfriendly environment's adverse effects on students' learning, career orientation, and critical thinking.

Desire and Church have explained how a learner's perception is affected directly or indirectly by the learning climate.

Strategies

Educators cannot force development but instead can only encourage it. If this development can be promoted, it can improve the course climate and make learning more conducive.

Universal principles can be formulated, and disciplinary approaches will remain useful.

To push students from Dualism, it is essential first to inspire uncertainty in their thinking. The learners need to bear the possibility to nurture flexibility and adaptability in their perceptions and approaches to problems.

Evidence is useful in promoting the learner from standard multiplicity.

To change their perspective from relativism, it is vital to study the consequences and relative values that are integrated with each process to give them full responsibility for their thinking processes.

The teachers should compare their perceptions regarding the course progress against the students' perspective since the course climate is all about proper understanding.

Responses to questions may differ, but these disparities can be sorted out.

The correlations between students and teachers are a significant determinant of the learning climate, mostly affecting the learners who are on the verge of quitting their study lines.

The teachers whom students feel as being more open, approachable, helpful, and friendly create better and more inspiring earning climates.

A conducive learning climate can also be influenced by the relationships between students and fellow students.

This is mostly applicable in extensive courses whereby student-student interaction is limited.

The tutors are required to promote these student interactions through group associations and collaborative learning management systems to create better learning climates.

The tone of information delivery also affects the climate.

Different hues of expressing a similar point produce differences in the learner's perceptions of the course due to the tutor's approachability and appeal to help the student in learning.

This determines the student's willingness, especially in seeking further guidance from the tutor regarding the subject in question. This aspect mostly affects newer learners at various levels of education.

We need to know how to study and be flexible in our learning approaches to be self-directed students.

The key to a self-directed approach is through practicing meta-cognition.

This promotes independent and goal-oriented thinking and enables self-reflection of one's learning activities.

Achieving this understanding requires developing "executive functioning" strategies, which allows one to be in charge of own thinking processes.

Meta-cognition entails planning, monitoring, and evaluation of the student's learning and perceptive abilities.

The learner in this stage can practice self-reflection and is aware of the limits of the known and unknown factors in their study.

The students are also equipped with plenty of learning abilities that they can apply in the process, including determining how and when to use the concepts and the adaptability to change of strategy if either approach fails.

They can analyze their results, highlight mistakes and errors in their work, and practice the newly learned procedures to tackle the next challenges.

According to the findings of Ambrose, Bridges, Dippier, Lovett, and Norman, the responsibility that the student has to be a self-directed learner is to learn how to make accurate assessments of the requirements of each task and evaluations of their acquired skills and knowledge.

They also need to strategize their approaches and adjust to strategy in different situations while monitoring their progress.

Research has long identified such behavior as a possible academic success indicator at all academic levels.

With the increased learning demands at the college level, it is essential to have learning approaches that transcend passive knowledge and memorization.

In most cases, students are seen as unprepared to apply the meta-cognitive strategies applied in college levels of education.

This factor applies even to accomplished students, especially those who grew without enough challenging situations, which are vital for developing meta-cognitive abilities.

Research shows that these skills are acquired best in the context of the courses.

Once learning methods are combined with the content, the learner can efficiently translate them to tasks and monitor that translation outcome.

By integrating different metacognitive strategies in the course work, instructors greatly assist students in developing their thinking processes.

Planning for Learning

For learning to be effective, the initial focus should be on planning. Accomplished students spend a great deal of time and resources during the planning process, an effort whose importance is hardly realized by the novice learners. Students should learn the importance of prior planning during the learning process.

Smart Decision Thinking

Problem-solving is that term that has found its place in most fields.

For example, in psychology, problem-solving would be defined as finding a solution to any mental issues or processes.

In contrast, statistics would be described as a method to answer a specific question on how many fish are there in a lake.

One must remember that the problems can also be categorized.

These categories would be well-defined and ill-defined problems.

Ill-defined problems, as the name suggests, are problems that do not have a clear-cut goal. It makes it challenging to come up with solutions to such issues.

You might not be able to identify an expected answer.

These problems have well-defined goals, making it easier to estimate the problem's magnitude and identify feasible solutions to the same.

We might also be able to plan if we recognize such a problem.

When you are faced with a problem in any field, or even in your life, you might either solve the problem through logic or try to interpret the question.

No matter which method you use, you have to first understand the problem's goal and try to identify the different routes you can take to solve the problem.

This is the key to problem-solving!

You might sometimes have to resort to abstract thinking and try coming up with a creative solution.

For instance, consider that you teach a bunch of 10-year-old English.

You have to cover the different parts of speech in an hour.

You know that the children that you teach have a low attention span.

Your problem here is to grab the kids' attention for an hour to help them understand the parts of speech.

You could either go about regularly teaching them using the text or make fun of them! This is a problem where you would use abstract thinking to find a creative solution.

You know that your children love games.

So, you can come up with a brilliant game that they will enjoy. But ensure that this game also teaches them the parts of speech!

Critical thinking is a knowledgeable skill, and it can benefit those who become adept at using it in every decision they make.

As a critical thinker, one of your goals is to become more familiar with your subconscious mind and learn about the knowledge base mechanics that resides there.

Critical thinkers know that arguments are created in such a way for people to have means of determining the validity of everything that happens in the world.

In most situations, you may not even know whether you could make the whole argument in proving that a claim is valid or not.

However, the way you argue would be the one that would count.

Problem Solver Qualities

Be Open-Minded

Do not go into a situation to be the 'hero' or 'savior.'

This will only serve to cloud your judgment because you will take it upon yourself to provide all the solutions.

A critical thinker knows that his or his approach is not the only one, and it may not be the best; hence, it is the importance of being open-minded.

When you are open-minded, you will listen to others and seek solutions that will work best, even when the answers are not something you provided.

Empathetic

To improve your problem-solving skills, you must look outside yourself.

Empathy allows you to do this; it removes internal focus from your biases and shifts it towards someone else.

When this happens, you begin to see situations through the eyes of someone else as it were. If you are empathetic, you will also improve your communication skills, your people skills (cooperation with other people), and your ability to work with others.

Employ Rational Considerations

Problem-solving should not use emotions, faulty, or incomplete information as to its basis.

Instead, it should use rational considerations as its base.

This means that you need to find out what is truly going on and gather all information before making any judgments.

Your solutions should use facts and evidence as to their base.

Your own opinion and emotions should not hinder your taste.

Problem-solving simply entails finding solutions to different situations, problems, and challenges you face.

It is an extremely crucial skill to build and improve because practical problem solving helps you combat challenges, ease your struggles, and find innovative fixes to the most bizarre and seemingly unfixable problems.

Besides, problem-solving is a lifesaver when it comes to making decisions.

If your problem-solving skills are excellent, you will likely make a well-thought-out and foolproof decision quickly and easily.

Nobody has excellent problem-solving skills at birth; we learn these skills and build them over time.

Smart Decisions

Personal Decision-Making Styles

Directive Style

If your decision-making style is directive, it means you value structure above all else. You are aggressive and expect instant results whenever you give an order.

When you encounter a problematic situation, you take charge, make fast decisions,

As a directive decision-maker, you have learned to depend entirely on your experience, knowledge, judgment, and information. You are a perfectionist for the rules and have excellent verbal skills to give clear directions.

However, there are some limitations to this style of making decisions.

You tend to act very quickly without waiting for all the facts.

This means that you are likely to make rash decisions without assessing other alternatives.

It is also possible that your choices provide short-term benefits but no long-term solutions.

Analytic Style

If this is your style of making decisions, then you are a born problem-solver.

You just love examining all kinds of problems, challenges, and puzzles and figuring them out.

You are innovative and enjoy dealing with large quantities of data whenever required to make a decision. Analysis-paralysis means nothing to you.

No matter how challenging the problem is, you are adaptable enough to handle it all.

On the flip side, however, you are also a slow decision-maker. You tend to wait for all the data and events to come in before making a move means your decision-making process can be very time-consuming.

To some extent, some people may describe you as a control freak.

Conceptual Style

As a conceptual decision-maker, you see problems from an artistic perspective. You tend to be very creative when solving problems.

You try as much as possible to come up with solutions that are fresh and new.

Unlike a directive decision-maker, you believe that every solution must be long-term.

You try to think about how your current decisions will impact the future.

As a result, you are a risk-taker and extremely achievement-oriented.

Behavioral Style

You are a natural peacemaker who believes that every decision must bring people together and avoid conflict.

You are very diplomatic and excel at persuading people to see your point of view. Since you are a people-person, you prefer to work in a group to agree on the best action to take.

This allows you to help people reconcile their differences and agree on one acceptable solution.

Group Decision-Making Styles

Autocratic Style

This is a decision-making style where you, as the leader of a group, take total control of every decision.

You don't even bother to ask your group members for their opinion or ideas on how to solve the problem.

You simply decide what to do, depending on your perception and internal information. As a result, you are held entirely responsible for your decision's positive and negative outcomes.

The autocratic style of decision-making is instrumental when the group needs to make a quick decision, for example, during an emergency.

However, this style also brings many challenges within the group.

Group members may not be enthusiastic about implementing a decision that was made without their input.

For example, if the decision affects employees negatively, morale will go down, and they will become resentful toward the manager.

Therefore, the company's productivity will be affected, and the manager may no longer be seen as a credible leader.

Democratic Style

This particular style allows you to make quick decisions by involving the entire group. As the leader, you give up your control and ownership of decision-making and enable group members to vote.

The resolution that gets the majority of the vote will be adopted and implemented by everyone.

The problem with this style is that, unlike the autocratic style, there is no sense of individual responsibility. No single member can be held responsible for any decision the group makes.

If something goes wrong, one member may refuse to accept responsibility because they voted against the resolution in the first place.

Collective Style

This is where the leader of a group gets everyone's input about the situation and involves the members in every step of the process.

However, the final decision rests with you alone.

You encourage your group members to share their ideas and any information they may have about the situation.

As they do this, you gain greater insight and a wide range of perspectives on how the problem may be solved. You analyze the input you have received and make your decision.

In the characteristic style of group decision-making, you have to accept full responsibility for the outcome of your decision.

The benefit of this style is that everyone gets the chance to participate in the process. To succeed as a leader, you must develop excellent communication skills and become a good listener.

This is the best technique for you to get a clear picture of the situation and make the best decision possible. On the other hand, the fact that you have to wait for group input makes the decision-making process very slow.

Consensus Style

This is quite similar to the democratic style, but what makes them different is that the decision must be unanimous in the consensus style of decision-making.

As a leader, you have no control over the final decision and do not have to accept individual responsibility for the outcome.

Everyone must agree. Otherwise, the decision cannot be regarded as consensual.

The most important value of this style is that it creates a strong sense of commitment within the group.

Everyone feels like their opinion matters and plays a part in the success of the group.

By involving every single member of the group, you will increase the likelihood of achieving success.

The consensual decision-making style is usually used when you have a small group of people working together for an extended period.

An excellent example of this is a business partnership.

The only downside is that the decision-making process will be slow.

It is also challenging to teach a group of people to work together like this and still maintain harmony.

Places to Intervene in A System

There are numerous places for systems thinkers that help out in almost any scenario.

While many of them have been discussed in abstract ways throughout the book, this Segment will focus on the specific categories of places and some methods to use them effectively.

While all of these places can easily stand alone, they also work very effectively in cooperation with one another in the spirit of systems thinking.

There are four broad categories of systems thinking places, from the familiar to the innovative. Brainstorming places are ones that most of us have used at one time or another during our academic years or professional lives.

Dynamic thinking places are also familiar to us, even if the name is not; these are the looping diagrams that show relationships and interactions between elements. Occasionally, these are reminiscent of a coach's description of a team's strategic plays.

Essential thinking places are graphs and diagrams that lay the foundation for more complex models, such as our last category.

Computer-based places are technological aides that run the gamut from learning laboratories to flight simulators; Simultaneously, these require high proficiency levels to create, they are efficiently utilized by anyone who has adequate training.

Brainstorming places are used in the early stages of creating a system or diagnosing a problem within an existing system.

One of the simple of these is something that almost every English teacher at one point in time encourages his students to do: the cluster diagram.

This layout places the central topic in the middle of a page and then has the individual or group associate ideas around the clusters' central one.

This is the organization's initial stage, wherein you are identifying the common elements within a particular system. From there, you can begin to see patterns and interrelationships.

Another brainstorming tool that can help see interactions and overlaps among parts is the old-school Boolean tool (this is the logic on which most search engines operate).

Usually depicted as two interlocking circles, wherein there is one idea to the left, one idea to the right, and a middle piece where the two meet and overlap.

This kind of model allows you to explore the relationship between two concepts: is it an "and" relationship? An "or" relationship? A "not" relationship? Searching for African "and" American will yield quite different results than searching for African "not" Americans, to use quite a general example.

This tool helps you define the parameters of the system you intend to utilize.

It can also be extended into interlocking circle designs, wherein you see the complexities of the interactions among many different terms and parts.

Dynamic thinking places go beyond simple linear graphs to show how events and information work in multi-directional ways. For example, a "behavior over time" graph charts different variables to explain how A, B, C, and so on interact with one another over some time.

A causal loop diagram can be used in conjunction with the "behavior over time" graph to chart how reinforcing and balancing loops work within the system.

A systems archetype diagram is the visual equivalent of explaining the dynamic interactions within complex systems: many of these have been explored within the book, such as drifting goals fixes that fail and shifting the burden.

These archetypes are most useful in identifying the fundamental source of a problem rather than responding to the immediate symptom.

Essential thinking places include graphical function diagrams, which show how one variable affects another, plotting the full range of relevant interactions over time and within context.

The policy structure diagram, which essentially maps the decision-making processes within an organization, can structure an entire organization and allocate resources within it.

Another example of an essential thinking tool is the structure-behavior pair, which provides the building blocks for the computer-based places.

These can include exponential growth, S-shaped growth, and other models that are genuinely three dimensional.

Computer-based places allow us to map out what we would like our system to look like and make predictions based on variable factors and play them out in virtual time.

These allow you to run policy analyses of long-term projects and project growth and resource needs. There are also the flight simulator models geared toward training management to deal with the company's every day running and the potential crisis that crops up.

Last, learning laboratories combine most of the systems thinking places within a computer simulation to train interactively.

Collaborative ways of thinking and working take time and creating a system that encapsulates the methodologies of systems thinking is a process, not an event. There are two fundamental ways to respond to an ever-changing world: when events happen, you can react, or, with knowledge of how functions work, you can be a participating actor instead of a passive reactor. When a machine breaks down, we respond by trying to fix it. With systems thinking, you begin to develop an ability to predict when and why the machine will break down, therefore giving yourself an edge in strategic planning and decision making. With these places at your disposal, your ability to transform your organization or your worldview is enabled.

Creating Change-In Systems

To understand how best to plan for the future, it is imperative to understand how systems behave. Among the most superficially different operation types, there are underlying systemic behaviors that we can discern common to most.

Indeed, feedback loops are a crucial part of that commonality. There are lessons to be learned about how to decode a system by witnessing other networks' failures and how feedback loops contribute to that process. On its surface, feedback is a simple concept:

listen to the stakeholders within the system to see what might be changed to better the system.

However, understanding feedback within complex systems requires a little more exploration.

To use some generalized examples, we have all witnessed the collapse of an initially hugely successful business that seems to implode overnight.

Or, we have seen (or participated in) the endless cycle of weight loss and weight gain, the same fifteen or twenty pounds gained and lost in a frustrating loop.

Or, we have struggled to host a Thanksgiving dinner devoid of negative family interactions.

At least one of these scenarios will ring a familiar bell for most of us.

These very different examples all contain certain commonalities, particularly the various feedback loops that either set us up to succeed or lead to failure.

The two feedback loops crucial to understanding systems are reinforcing loops and balancing loops. Indeed, these are the very building blocks of dynamic systems structures.

In the case of reinforcing loops, we find that these contribute to both positive growths, and in many cases, eventual collapse.

This feedback loop begins positively by recognizing success within the system—the business is growing; profits are increasing—which encourages the system's parts to maintain the status quo.

Management, workers, the means of production are all reinforced to stay the same. Concomitantly, this means that growth and change are happening only in one direction. This is like having a savings account:

each month, the interest accrues you have positive growth in additional savings (this assumes you aren't withdrawing, of course).

However, this reinforcing loop can lead to sedentary behavior.

It's great that the savings account grows incrementally with monthly interest.

Still, it doesn't necessarily encourage you to invest more money into the said account or diversify said account to accrue more interest. Nevertheless, this positive growth is at least a movement in the right direction.

When reinforcing loops grow truly stagnant, though, as, within an organization, it fails to notice changes that require new and different responses, for example, if a company creates a product that is suddenly in high demand, then the company must respond to this not by reinforcing the same behaviors that led to that demand.

In fact, without changes to the means of production and distribution, this can lead to underproduction and, eventually, a reputation for not reliably meeting demand. (Paradoxically, scarcity can sometimes increase demand.)

It can also lead to complacency wherein the original best-selling item is redesigned by a competitor who has been more carefully watching the market, thus rendering your product obsolete.

Just because your innovative system produced success doesn't mean that it will continue to do so without further developing ideas and investment of resources.

With balancing loops, the system is encouraged to reach a state of stability, wherein demand does not outstrip supply, nor does the amount overwhelm demand.

These balancing loops take us out of reinforcing loops' linear thinking, where the outcomes are increased growth or slow decline.

Balancing loops work multi-directionally and encourage communication at and between every level.

When a system is in balance, it has the original goal of achieving a specific performance level.

Tesla is an example of a company that has appeared to be recently out of balance, promising mid-priced cars by a particular date without having the strategic planning in place to deliver—too few workers and assembly lines that were overworked for too long.

Tesla grew too fast to make good on its promises.

A system in balance is one in which a strategic plan is explicitly articulated in the service of a particular vision. Indeed, what fuels the balancing loop is the gap between the ideal goals and the actual performance; thus, you need clear goals and clear strategies even to begin to recognize the differences.

The system is built to be self-reinforcing, like a thermostat in your house:

when the air is cold enough or warm enough, the system shuts itself off until the desired temperature starts to drop or rise restarts itself, maintaining a reasonably constant temperature.

This is how an ideally balanced system works.

Balancing systems are common in nature and human-designed systems, but we don't always notice them because they are quietly keeping things in a happy balance.

When we begin to see problems, we recognize that something in the system is flawed enough to interrupt the balancing loops. This is when we speak of "damage control":

something has disrupted the normal flow of events. We must step in to analyze the system to determine which parts are no longer contributing to the system's overall function.

The other important element within the idea of balancing feedback loops is that it encourages better and more egalitarian communication.

Instead of managers and board members calling all the shots about how the system is set up, the workers and producers are also called upon to give their perspectives.

Diversifying the feedback will assist in identifying the gaps within the system before they lead to irreversible damage.

For example, a worker on the production line might suggest that they slow down production; from his perspective, the work is too fast-paced, or the output is too large for the shrinking demand.

She might suggest that they invest more resources into hiring more production line workers or improving the line's efficiency for a manager.

The worker knows the conditions on the ground, as it were, while the manager is more aware of the resources that can be allotted to fix the gaps that are throwing the system out of balance. By working together, a long-term solution can finally be addressed.

Start Thinking

To start, let's look at how much you are thinking in general.

Whether we are going to work, perhaps even at work, cleaning, hanging out with friends, or doing whatever else, you might find that you are only thinking for a portion of this time.

Ray Crystal

not engaging in the rendering of legal, financial, medical or professional advice. The content within this book has been derived from various sources. Please consult a licensed professional before attempting any techniques outlined in this book.

By reading this document, the reader agrees that under no circumstances is the author responsible for any losses, direct or indirect, which are incurred as a result of the use of information contained within this document, including, but not limited to, — errors, omissions, or inaccuracies.

Introduction

Systems that think as they do in modern times have been around for approximately 60 years but have only had a relatively large audience among non-scientists within the last decade.

Thinking structures is a way to look at things, individuals, and organizations worldwide.

It consists of principles and methods that give system-thinkers a new, potentially expanding worldview rather than a series of static methodologies or theories.

Systems that think, also called systems thinking, is a school of thought drawn from multiple disciplines, including systems theory in the natural and social sciences, research on human knowledge representation, linguistics, philosophy, psychology, cognitive science, management science, architecture, and organizational design, cybernetics, computers, and software development.

Thinking structures encourages observation-based, practical, and creative thinking, instead of that which is inferred from theories, formulas, rules, or Logic.

Here are the four principles that form the essence of thinking structures:

1. Thinking structures are sets of principles and methods that together give system-thinkers a new, potentially expanding worldview.

2. Not all systems thinking is the same. Systems represent things, activities, and properties. Systems exist

at different levels. How these systems are interconnected differ? To be effective, systems thinking must be sensitive to the different ways in which these systems interconnect.

3. Thinking structures are an alternative to thinking methods, which, as methods, prescribe instead of providing principles and methods for thinking about individuality, organizations, and society.

4. Thinking methods are constants.

Thinking structures are metaphors.

In some way, structures don't exist objectively and rely on the human observer to see entities or processes as structures.

However, it can be beneficial to consider events in the world as structures and make sense of their behavior.

Thinkers of structures prefer to consider the environment as a series of ongoing interactions, changes, and processes.

Systems analysis, in a way, complements the instrumental view offered by mainstream reductionist science.

Thinking structures are by no means a limited set of rules or formulas. They offer ways of seeing experience in new and provocative ways.

Systems thinking about any particular event can lead to unexpected conclusions. Such negative results are typical in science.

To overcome them, however, theories are always built on a reliable foundation of knowledge. Neither reductionist science nor systems thinking rely on formulas. There are three significant differences between them.

First, reductionist science is a way of representing reality in a formulaic form. Systems thinking is by no means a straitjacket.

Second, systems thinking is not just a hypothesis about the world that is

validated by evidence. It is an alternative
to thinking scientifically.

**Third, science sees entities as static,
isolated, and independent.**

However, systems-thinkers see entities as
structures in a context and acknowledge
that their behavior is to an unknown
extent variable and mostly unpredictable.

Thoughts about structures are always
changeable and reliant on interpretations
- even after centuries, new facts and

evidence can cause old theories to be replaced.

Throughout the book, we will look at various archetypes of typical ways in which systems function, and more importantly, how they become dysfunctional over time if we don't examine how the dynamic works.

This allows us to look beyond mere events to the patterns of behavior within the system itself that lead up to them. It's a powerful mechanism wherein we

become active instead of reactive to
events as they occur.

Understanding the dynamic can be a very
constructive way of leading us to a new
behavioral and cognitive ability to assess
circumstances from the systems point of
view instead of a systematic approach to
problem-solving.

How to Improve Your Thoughtful?

Most of it lies dormant within us, or it is underdeveloped. Any development in thinking cannot take place if there is no mindful commitment to learning.

You cannot improve your game in basketball if you don't put in some effort to do so, and the same is true for critical thinking.

Like any other skill, the effort is essential for its development. As long as you take your thinking for granted, there is no way in which you can unlock your true potential.

Development in your thinking process is gradual, and there are several plateaus of learning that you will have to overcome, and hard work is a precondition for all of this. You cannot become an excellent thinker by just wanting to become one.

You will have to make an aware decision to change certain habits, which will take some time. So, be patient and don't expect any change to occur overnight.

Stage 1:

You are still unaware of the significant problems or pitfalls in your thinking. You aren't a reflective thinker. Most of us are stuck in this stage.

Stage2:

You start developing awareness of the problems in your thinking.

Stage 3:

You try working on your thought
processes, but not regularly.

Stage 4:

You realize the need for regular practice.

Stage 5:

You start noticing a change in the way
you think.

Stage 6:

You develop the ability to become
insightful in your thinking.

You can progress through these stages by
accepting the fact that there are specific

problems in the way you think, and you start putting in conscious effort to improve yourself.

Making Use of "Wasted" Time

All human beings tend to waste time. That is, we fail to make productive use of all the time we have at our disposal. Sometimes we flit from one form of diversion to another without actually enjoying any of them.

At times we get irritated about matters that are clearly beyond our control.

At times, we don't plan well, which causes a butterfly effect of negative consequences that could all have been easily avoided by simple planning.

Apart from all the time that we waste doing nothing, we start worrying about unnecessary things. Sometimes we regret how we functioned in the past, or we just end up daydreaming about "what could have been" and "what can be" instead of putting in some effort to achieve results. You need to know that there is no way you can get all the lost time back again.

Instead, try focusing on all the time that you have at your disposal now.

One way you can develop the habit of critical thinking is to use the time that would have normally been "wasted." Instead of outlay an hour in front of the TV flipping through channels and getting bored, you can make use of this time or at least a part of it for reflecting on the day you had, the tasks you accomplished, and all that you need to achieve.

Spend this time to contemplate your productivity. Here are a questions that you can ask yourself:

When did I do my worst and best thinking today? What was it that I was thinking about all day long? Did I manage to come to a logical conclusion, or was it all in vain?

Did I indulge in any negative thinking? Did the negative thoughts just create a lot of unnecessary frustration?

If I could repeat this day all over again, what would I change?

Did I do something that will help me in achieving my goals? Did I accomplish anything worth remembering?

Spend some time answering these questions and record your observations. Over some time, you will notice that you have a specific pattern of thinking.

Internalizing Intellectual Standards

Every week select any one of these standards and try to increase your awareness of the same. For instance, you can focus on clarity for a week, then shift towards precision, and so on.

If you can focus on clarity, observe how you communicate with others, and see for yourself if you are clear or not.

Also, notice when others aren't being clear in what they are saying.

Whenever you are reading, see if you are clear about the content you have been reading.

While expressing yourself orally or writing your thoughts down, check for yourself if there is some precision in what you are trying to convey.

There are four simple things that you can make use of to test whether you have some clarity or not.

You have to explicitly state what you are trying to say, elaborate on it, give examples for facilitating better understanding, and make use of analogies as well.

So, you are supposed to state, then elaborate, illustrate, and lastly exemplify yourself.

Maintain an Intellectual Journal

Start maintaining an intellectual journal where you record specific information every week. Here is the raw format that you should follow.

The first step is to list down the situation that was or is significant to you emotionally. It should be something that you care about, and you need to focus on one situation.

After this, record your response to that
situation.

Try being as specific and accurate as you
can.

Once you have done this, your necessity
to analyze your reaction and analyze
what you have written.

The final step is to assess what you have
been through.

Assess the implications - what have you
learned about yourself?

Reshaping Your Character

Select intellectual trait-like perseverance, empathy, independence, courage, humility, and so on. Once you have selected a feature, try to focus on it for an entire month and cultivate it in yourself.

If the trait you have opted for is humility, start noticing whenever you admit that you are wrong.

Notice if you refuse to admit this, even if the evidence points out that you are wrong.

Notice when you start becoming defensive when someone tries to point out your mistake or make corrections to your work.

Observe when your arrogance prevents you from learning something new, whenever you notice yourself indulging in any form of negative behavior or thinking squash such thoughts. Start reshaping your character and start˙ incorporating desirable behavioral traits while giving up on the negative ones.

You are your worst enemy, and you can prevent your growth unknowingly. So, learn to let go of all things negative.

Dealing with Your Egocentrism

Human beings are inherently selfish.

While thinking about something, we tend to favor ourselves before anyone else subconsciously.

Yes, we are biased towards ourselves.

You can notice your selfish behavior daily by thinking about the following questions:

What are the situations under which you would favor yourself?

Whenever you feel egocentric, think about what a rational person would say or do in a similar situation and compare to what you are doing.

Redefining How You See Things

The world that we live in is social as well as private, and every situation is "defined."

How a situation is defined determines how you feel and the way you act, and its implications.

However, every situation can be described in multiple ways.

This means that you have the power to make yourself happy and your life more fulfilling.

This means that all those situations you attach to a negative meaning can be transformed into something favorable if you want it to.

This strategy is about finding something positive in everything that you would have considered to be negative.

Try to see the silver lining in every aspect of your life.

It is all about perspectives and perceptions.

If you think that something is positive, you will feel good about it, and if you think it's negative, you will naturally harbor negative feelings towards it.

Get in Touch with Your Emotions

Whenever you start feeling some negative emotion, ask yourself the following:

What line of thinking has led to this emotion?

For instance, if you are angry, ask yourself, what were you thinking about that caused your anger?

What are the further ways in which I can view this situation?

Every situation seems different, depending on your perspective.

A negative aspect makes everything seem dull and bleak and, on the other hand, a positive outlook does brighten things up.

Whenever you feel a negative emotion creeping up, try to see some humor in it or rationalize it.

Concentrate on the thought process that produced the negative emotion, and you can find a solution to your problem.

Analyzing the Influence of a Group on Your Life

Carefully observe the way your behavior is influenced by the group you are in.

For instance, any group will have specific unwritten rules of conduct that all the members follow.

There will be some form of conformity that will be enforced.

Check for yourself how much this influences you and how it impacts you.

Check if you are bowing too much to the pressure being exerted and doing something just because others expect it.

You don't have to start practicing all the steps at once.

Start slowly and try following as many as you can.

Primarily, you will need to put in a conscious effort for critical thinking to work and, over a period, these skills will come naturally to you.

Start Thinking

To start, let's look at how much you are thinking in general.

Whether we are going to work, perhaps even at work, cleaning, hanging out with friends, or doing whatever else, you might find that you are only thinking for a portion of this time.

When you are thinking, you might find that you have trouble sorting through your thoughts, or they are not relevant to the task.

In this Segment we'll talk about the wasted time you have in your schedule for mindless purposes. Some things do not require thinking.

It is usually obvious which types of activities require thinking and which do not.

If you spend time cleaning a stove, for example, you may have noticed that not much thinking is needed here.

You identify what needs to be done (scrubbing the surfaces and using cleaning materials to clean the mess), and you do it.

Another example is walking the dog.

The dog needs to get some exercise (so do you), so you take it outside, put on its leash, and walk for a bit. Not much thinking here.

However, there are a couple of strategies to change this wasted time into valuable critical thinking time.

One aspect of this is that when there is the context around these mindless tasks, it may be necessary to use critical thinking skills to make them easier or more efficient.

For example, you need to cook the pot roast at 1 PM, and it will take until 5 PM to complete the cooking process. Should you schedule the cleaning time before or after this process?

This depends on a couple of factors; you will need to address your schedule for the day and think about how long it takes to clean the stove, and what the effect of cleaning the furnace will have on your physical and mental state, as well as coming up with a strategy to be an effective cleaner. The dog likes to be walked in the morning;

if he is, he acts more relaxed throughout the day.

You have a busy morning, so you must figure out a strategy to get the dog walked in the morning, as this is the optimal time to walk the dog while still addressing your needs and goals along the way.

Another strategy is to use scheduled thinking times for your mindless tasks.

If you have a dog walk planned for 8 AM, for twenty minutes, find a way to incorporate some critical thinking into this time frame.

For twenty minutes, you can sort through personal problems or things that have been holding you back.

You can set yourself a schedule of thinking throughout the day that will compartmentalize your cognitive tasks.

This is easier said than done; we tend to slip into mindlessness.

You must face this tendency and use intentionality to overcome it.

What does this mean?

It involves at least some measure of self-talk. Self-talk is what you say to yourself in your mind.

It isn't a verbally "talking" to oneself, but somewhat self-directed thoughts were characterizing our attitudes toward ourselves and our internal drives. Self-talk can go a little something like this:

"I am starting to think about Betty at work. She is so annoying. Every day, when I go to get my coffee, it seems that she tries to get there before me so that she is assured a cup of coffee, even if I'm not."

You want to shift this away from this type of thinking. Try to go down this route: "Betty usually arrives at the office at 9:30 AM.

If I get to the office at nine and make my pot of coffee, I can avoid this problem altogether." Self-talk is necessary to route your mind away from the petty thoughts that it tends to gravitate toward and send you into a more productive headspace.

Self-talk is critical; it's a tool that will be very useful in solving problems and applying critical thinking skills. You can think of self-talk as one of the pillars of critical thinking.

Each of us has "voices." This is not to say that we suffer from delusions or hallucinations, but rather that we have different ways of talking to ourselves in different moments. It can be helpful to identify and manage your self-talk by analyzing what you're saying to yourself.

Some people have voices that tell them they are not right or that they have many negative attributes that they must focus on.

These voices may sound something like this:

"You are no good. You can't do that. You've never done that before; you will mess up if you try."

This is the first layer of self-talk that you must defeat before developing your ability for critical thinking.

If you have these types of voices that speak to you, try to talk back. Tell them, "I am good enough. I know how to try new things.

If there is something that I want to do that is just out of reach, it is possible to overcome my challenges and reach what I need." This voice that speaks back to the initial self-talk should be gentle and reasonable.

It should keep in mind the realistic expectations that are appropriate for the moment.

It might take some time to identify the various voices of self-talk included in your psyche; for some, they are challenging to disagree with.

Some people have internalized these voices so much that they never question their self-talk. These kinds of people will have difficulty with critical thinking and problem-solving.

Being aware of oneself is an art and a science. Let's talk about both. Awareness can be art because, sometimes, the way that you can express what is going on with you can't be summarized in words.

Sometimes, it is a feeling, an image, or a habit of thinking.

Awareness of yourself may come in fleeting moments; you may be gazing upon a beautiful vista when you realize that your mind is uncontrolled to the degree that you desire, and that moment can be beautiful.

Being aware of oneself can come through artistic pursuits, such as writing or making art or music.

These activities can help you become more aware of the cognitive processes in your life as well as emotional processes.

You can sort out the moving from the cognitive and realize what needs to be shifted in your processing. There may be some tremendous emotional block to

getting your mind into critical thinking.
Where could this have come from?

It may have come from an overbearing
parent, who pressured you when
problem-solving situations were nigh. It
could've come from a particular
experience or association you have with
whatever situation you are facing.

Connecting with nature, people, or art
can help you make connections and
become aware of when you are thinking
and when you are not.

If we think about becoming aware of oneself as a science, we can think about how we can monitor our thinking. You may find it useful to write things down and keep lists. Many people like to write their thoughts out in different formats to become aware of what's going on in mind. You can keep count of how many negative views you have in 12 hours, for example.

This is a scientific formula-based way to do an "experiment" on yourself to gain insight.

Here's a way you could format this experiment. For one week, without changing anything, record your negative thoughts.

Every time you have one, make a mark on a piece of paper. Have the paper divided into one piece for each day of the week and try to specify when these negative thoughts arose during the week.

At the finale of the week, you will have many data.

Now comes the time to be a scientist.

Go back through the week and try to describe what happened each day.

Look for examples of times when you had excessive negative thoughts.

You can find reasons and triggering situations in this method.

Once you have identified the circumstances in which the negative thoughts arose, you can start to become aware of how your mind is working and what you need to do to eliminate those thoughts.

For example, maybe you'll notice that when you wake up, the chronic pain in your foot makes you take a long-time eating breakfast.

Then, your mind went into self-blame mode, thinking, "I am always late because of this stupid situation."

You now have an objective perspective on this problem, and you can address your thinking appropriately.

Conclusion

Systems thinking is perhaps best defined as seeing possibilities in an ongoing, complex adaptive, physical systems.

Within complex adaptive systems, individuals and organizations do not operate as isolated parts, but work together in dynamic ways to create change, challenge, or sustain the status quo.

In our systems of modern industrialized society, these are complex adaptive systems.

Systems thinker conclude that there is a need for a shift in the very structure of society today.

To change our approach to change, we must become aware of the genuine differences within our societies and organizations and their interconnections.

Traditionally, we have been stuck with the practices of outdated tools such as the scientific and industrial revolution,

which have not been designed to last.

We have been led to believe that we can

somehow escape from the consequences

of limited resources, growing

technologies and limited space, however

now is the time to re-think our present

and future generations.

Our governing bodies, must be more

inclusive of their people and in particular

the younger generations.

As part of the rethinking we must have a shift in how we see ourselves.

Right now our modern systems can only duplicate a version of itself outwards.

In the future, we need to recreate more of the original in our ways, recognizing from within any particular part that the original system was a whole system with a life force.

This requires us to understand the generation cycle of any system, from its birth to its death.

This is so that we better understand the life cycles of the systems we are trying to create to understand how to avoid better the boxes that we often find ourselves trapped in and how to create in new ways.

We have to take a broader view of the life cycle of all the systems we are part of.

If we continue to be limited to thinking in terms of simple linear cause and effect chains, systems tend to behave in a way where one small change in a single place

is destined to cause a change

everywhere, for good or ill.

Instead we must become aware of the

more significant systems in which we

live, and how these give rise to form and

structure within all systems, and upon

which we can act and react.

As a result, we understand that many

different kinds of change can come from

the organized or unorganized actions in a

system.

We know that we must look at the political structures these actions take place in and understand the economy, social structures, and other systems.

This is only possible through systems thinking, where we take a fresh look at what it means to be human.

The person who has the most accurate model of reality and acts accordingly will win. Be that person, and beautiful things will happen to you shortly.

Taking charge of your life requires you first to take charge of your thoughts.

This s because ideas are the basis on which our behavior and lifestyles are formed.

Wrong thoughts lead to bad experiences and adverse outcomes, while good thoughts have the power to steer your life in a new positive direction.

CPSIA information can be obtained
at www.ICGtesting.com
Printed in the USA
BVHW061008210321
603119BV00004B/657